# *The failed painting of a heart*

**Liam Osaneo**

I would like to thank Megan Bowen for her incredibly valuable input on the script and Alana Nastold for her brilliant design of the cover.

*For Scrat,*
*who unknowingly made this book possible.*

Liam Osaneo was born in rural upper Bavaria in 1999 and is now living in Munich as a student after spending about a year abroad seeing many things and eating loads of instant noodles. Writing has always been a huge part of his live be it in poems, plays, short-stories or unfinished books and he doesn´t think that this will ever change. His work is mainly an attempt to honestly project what he sees thinks and feels. There is no big motivation or mission behind it other than that. He also has a blog on Write Out Loud where he publishes little bits of his work.

I wish I could be
one of those
motivational writers
that tell you positive things
make you feel better
lift your self-confidence
but the truth is
I don't have the slightest clue
I don't know
if love will come for you
some die alone
I don't know
if you are beautiful
some hearts are ugly
I don't know
if you will find meaning
most people don't
I can only tell you
the truths I found
along my path
and tell you the tale
of my struggles
and my successes
and all they taught me
With this book
you can look into a mirror
through my eyes
and see honestly
all that makes me
The ugliness
the beauty

the black
the white
the grey
all of it
that is my promise
to you
honesty

# Pieces of a mirror

You all were some part of me
a stone on my path
a step on my ladder
a punch in my face
it does not matter
You had an impact
you had enough force
enough character
to change me
form me
develop me
into what I am today
A dozen currents
steering a little boat
on a rushing stream
and a little man
sitting at the back
clutching the rudder

Can you give me
a huge black bird
that can take me by the neck
and lift me up
towards the midnight sky?
I feel like the stars
are lonely
and crying for help
I could save them
make them black
just like
the night around them
so they would finally
belong somewhere

Starlight on my soul
and my mind
branding me
creature of the night
night thoughts
night feelings
night heart
night light
no sunrise
in sight

I´ve always loved a bird
with a broken wing
better
than a healthy one
makes me
forgive myself
my own flaws
my own broken parts
Cause nothing can be crueler
than a beautiful perfect little bird

I know exactly
why I like black
in the clothes I wear
the car I drive
and the books I read
Black is the calmest colour
it doesn't yell
it doesn't complain
it doesn't argue
it just accepts
you
I need more black
in my life

Are you laughing
with me right now?
because
I feel like I can hear
your joy travelling
through the night
flying high
like a raven on cold wind
towards my bedroom window
But sadly
the bird crashed
and broke its neck
on the glass
Some distances
are too far
Ravens can die
of exhaustion

Stop staring at me
from inside these walls
stop listening to me
through the ceiling
I see you
all of you
watching every step I take
judging everything I make
Can I hide from you
if I put a strange skin
over my face
and steal
the way they walk
the way they talk
the way they breathe
If I cut a stranger open
and put his skin
around me
so no one can see
what hides inside
Strange eyes
looking at me in the mirror
judging me
but not reaching me

It takes me back
into another life
to sit back
in an empty café
listening to strange music
over a coffee I can´t afford
on a cold day
And just to look out of the window
watching people I don't know
and will never know
It gives me peace
makes me vanish
melting with this place
into some strange happy hybrid
a creature
made of background voices
a little music
a bit of coffee
and a few drops of ink
An animal that only exists
in certain places
at certain times

Cold and warm
is my heart
hard and soft
is my mind
A switch man
a change man
a clay man
is me
Look at me
and find out
who I become
when you are near
If I were a superhero
I would be mirror man

I was skinny
of course
my hair was a mess
I wore the same three shirts
every week
I didn´t shower for days
but it didn't matter
no one´s hair was perfect
everyone wore random stuff
we didn't always have showers
but we didn't care
we just looked around
and were enchanted
by the magic around us
such pure friendship
such pure joy
birthed by the simplest things
how could this not be
the way life was meant to be

write "me"
would you
it´s just two letters
not that much
of an effort
but if you repeat it
often enough
a thousand times
it might finally
mean something

Not in reality
do I walk through this forest
not in reality
do I hear these birds
or drink this cold water
of the morning leaves
I look up
and see the green sunlight
breaking through the concrete
finding me
in my little box
I wait here
patiently
until it takes me home

I see this man
wearing this black coat
in this empty café
I see him
clear as day
his empty look
his fading hair
his hanging shoulders
I see him
he just sits there
all by himself
staring into the rain
I just don't want him
to be me
one day

# Red drops

Through the sick and frozen mist
I see you walk
ripping it apart
with your bright red coat
and your bright red smile
A sad little dot
of some strange warmth
awakes inside me
when you walk by
And your shoes crush
the fallen leaves on the ground
as you leave behind
a trail of broken things
that whisper your name
A wonderful red light
getting swallowed by the mist
fading
with every step you take
I can fully understand
why he won´t let you go

Find a person
that doesn't make you
burn yourself for them
but soothes you
like cold water
on a fresh burn
Bring me peace
there is enough war
inside me

Are you
a myth?
Some fairy tale figure
made in my heart
Or do you breathe
do you have lungs
that suck in the air
and a heart pumping blood
through your veins
If I catch you
in the end
will I feel
soft warm skin
in my hands
Or a cloud of smoke
disappearing
through my fingers

Some parts of me
still remember
the way you felt
I would cut them open
if I could

I cannot wait forever
I cannot wait again
I cannot wait
too long
again
I can´t afford
to be late
this time
Not with you

We walk
at the same pace
our heads
face the same way
our thoughts
circle the same thing
But I don't turn
and neither do you
so we walk
Like two coins
rolling on their edges
not daring
to collide
cause they don't know
if they would fall
on the ground
or onto each other
I can still feel
my heart beating
painfully
in my chest
wondering
how a stranger got through my shell
so quickly
It´s rather sad
even a bit
humiliating
but at the same time
it´s also kind of magic

In fading light
I see you walk
along the street
You go steadily
into the mist
making it harder
and harder
for me to remember
what your face looked like

Mr and Mrs
took each other´s hands
and lay down
on the silk
A look
a nod
a tiny smile
And it all went bad
and the bed turned red
Not many people
at their funeral

For some people it´s in the eyes
or in the smile
or the way they toss their hair
For me it´s in the way
she raises her eyebrow
that's where my love is

you threw a stone
through my window
and watched the glass
fall down
in slow motion
and now I can´t fix it
and cold air is getting in
and I can´t ignore
the world outside
anymore

I want to dance again
holding someone warm
firmly in my hands

Forget me please
I scream at you
as you knock on my door
with tears in your eyes
in that black dress
once again
I hit you
with all my force
push you away
and slam that door
into you face
I hear you cry
in the rain
and I know
you´ll be back
I can´t kill
a memory

# Grey season thoughts

Could we reschedule please
I have no time
for love and support
at 5 pm tomorrow
I have a bit of stress and anger
to do
It would be better
on Wednesday at 6
it would fit perfectly
between disappointment earlier
and drunk excitement later on

Do the flowers
waiting in the ground
know about the spring?
do they know about
the sea of colours
they are about to become
or do they believe
they are just
trapped
in the frozen ground
in endless cold
and darkness
forever
Unable to scream
under the snow

There is a sex shop
on the other side of the street
with blinking red lights
and big screaming pictures
and I´m sitting here
with my coffee
and my book
well this is just great
now the city is mocking me too

Sometimes ugliness
is all you need
a little evil
a little hate
a little failure
in the people you love
just some black
in all their white
A little forgiveness

It´s easy to forget
the steam rising from your coffee
the smell of jelly
on fresh bread
and the sound of the birds
on a winter morning
When you sit alone
in your room
at night
it´s easy to forget

A sun for the shadows
is what I want
some light
and some warmth
for the dark corners of the world
where the ball of fire
that warms us
never shines
so that the creatures
that live in these
cold dark places
could stop to shiver and cough
and would stop haunting us
in our dreams

This is the moment
to run along the beach
in the middle of the night
at full speed
wearing nothing
but my trunks
Too bad I´m in a city
in February
and people give you strange looks
if you do that here

As long as there are people
that walk over cracking floors
while their fingers glide
over dusty covers
that soak in the smell
of the lives lived inside them
As long as there are people
that smile slightly
while trying to pick
There is hope
As long as there are bookshops
there is hope

Do trees
have memories
do they remember
the winters they´ve mastered
and the springs they´ve enjoyed?
Or do they suffer
every year
every fall
thinking they are dying
when the snow begins to fall?
Do they know
their leaves will regrow
and shine again in the brightest green?
Or do they cry for them
when they fall through their branches
like little drops of dying light
floating through stiff fingers?
Do the trees cry
every fall
and laugh
every spring?
or do they just sit there
and smile knowingly
at the everchanging world around them?

# Dark bits

I don't need you
to make me laugh
I know funny people
I don't need you
to hear me talk
I have an audience
I don't need you
for an argument
I´m surrounded by brilliant people
I need you
because my fingers
won´t stop trembling
and I keep panting
I need you
because my mind is
flickering
and won´t hold still
I need you
because my vision
keeps blurring
and I can´t see
I don´t need you
for my mind
I need you
for my soul

three faces
staring at me
through the concrete
three faces
condemning me
with iron eyes
one face
I starved
to death
one face
I stabbed
in the back
one face
I did not dare
to love
three faces
staring at me
through the concrete
three faces
watching me fall

Just lay your hand
in mine
when I´m shaking
because the frost
is running through my veins
Just lay your hand
in mine
when my eyes flicker
and all I can see
is darkness
Just lay your hand
in mine
you don't have to do
anything
you don't have to say
anything
Just lay your hand in mine
I just need to know
I´m not alone
out here
in the cold

They say
the pain will help you grow
that you will learn
from the experience
"what doesn't kill you makes you stronger"
they tell you
I say they are wrong
some pain
this pain
doesn't help, doesn't build
anything
It´s not a phase
you need to go through
to become stronger
it´s bleeding
that needs to be stopped
before it kills you

crush this
and that
and every little thing
break us all
until
there are only pieces left
in a shattered world

I know that I will suffer
I know there will be times
when I can only see
the night around me
and forget there is light
I know
this part of me
will never fully go away
this black dog
following me around
I know these things
But I also know
I also learned
that I can bear
that I have the strength
and the fire
in my heart
not to stop
or pass it on
to the people that love me
but to walk with it
holding it on a leash
like the loyal old friend
it is

Calm me
wrap your hands
around my shaking soul
and pull it close
towards your heat
Drive out this cold
that makes me shiver
alone in my bed
and put me gently
into yours
Heat my life

Follow me through the night
my black dog
you will be
my companion
I can feel
your cold wet nose
touching my hand
as we walk
on broken leaves
in the midnight forest

# A blind man´s opinion on picasso

Trust me
you'll be fine
you've been through worse than this
mastered harder challenges
overcome greater obstacles
beaten bigger enemies
and never once
have you truly given up
never once
did you truly fail to find your way
and do you know why?
Cause that little fire
burning in your chest
refuses to go out
and keeps fighting
and keeps going
and keeps you running
and keeps you winning
one way or another
and does it really matter
when each and every one
of your many successes happen?
you don't have to be afraid
you don't have to cry
sooner or later
your dreams will come true
they might just change a little bit
along the way
Trust me

Hold up your torch
and shine a light
into another person
instead of only
into yourself

Always remember
there is enough darkness
in all of us

There never will be
stillness
on your path
There will never be
silence
in your heart
in the same way
there will never be
pausing
a river
or slowing
a  stream
You are the struggle
you are the movement
you are the noise
you are the fire

Some days run over you
coughing and panting
with sweat dripping
from their skin
leaving deep footprints
on your ground
While other days
try to sneak over you
barefoot
smooth as silk
not making a scratch
on your surface
The kind of days you need
depends on how much
you need your world to change

to those stumbling
through a maze
of decisions
and endless options
unable to find the exit
I tell you breathe
sit down
just stay wherever you are
You will feel
the walls fading
eventually

Just believe me
if I tell you
to believe in yourself
But don't ever
believe yourself
if you don't
believe in yourself
You just have to
believe yourself
when you believe in yourself
and don't believe yourself
when you don't believe
in yourself
It´s easy
believe me

Why are you not
ridiculous when you can
not childish
when it´s inappropriate
not unreasonable
when its important
a surprise
to your mind
a dancing child
that sings
of magic things
and pushes serious people
far  away

# At the dinner table

My point is not
to convince you
nor is it
to tell you something
I just want to
see you smile
and hear us talk about
some sweet memories
let´s not spoil that
with substance
I tell you nothing
and you don't reply
so no one shouts

We speak every day
but haven't talked in ages
Cause you don't know
that I can handle
to see you in pain
and you don't always
have to be
strong for me

We sit at the table together
and we speak but don't say a word
and yet I don't
but I want to
I can't

# reasons

For the warm sun
on your face
on a cold winter morning
For the song of the birds
and the sound of the trees
For the calmness
of the mountains
and the wisdom
of the lakes
And for that little late sparrow
searching for crumbs

Cause there are mornings
beautiful mornings
mornings full of laughter
and the smell of good coffee
mornings we spend together
when friendship
and love
sit together on the breakfast table
Mornings we forget
far too quickly
as the day goes by

For the way you hug me
when we see each other again
The look on your face
when you make me laugh
The way you listen
and surprise me
with tiny gifts
The safety of this place
the wounds we healed together
the scars we wear
together

Cause I want to kiss
the right lips
And I haven't found them yet

For the sun
shining through my window
warming my face
Promising me
a day of light

Cause there still are
Books to be read
plays to be seen
movies to be watched
friends to be found
loves to bc loved
Pieces of joy
to be collected

for the fading light
between night and day
the thin border
between two worlds
where light breathes out
and darkness in

cause we seldom are
as alone
as we think we are
we just get so used
to some people
that we think
they don't count
anymore
they do

What a warm feeling it is
to hold the happiness
of someone you love
firmly in your hands
To gently put it
into their hearts
and watch their smile light up

Thank you for reading.